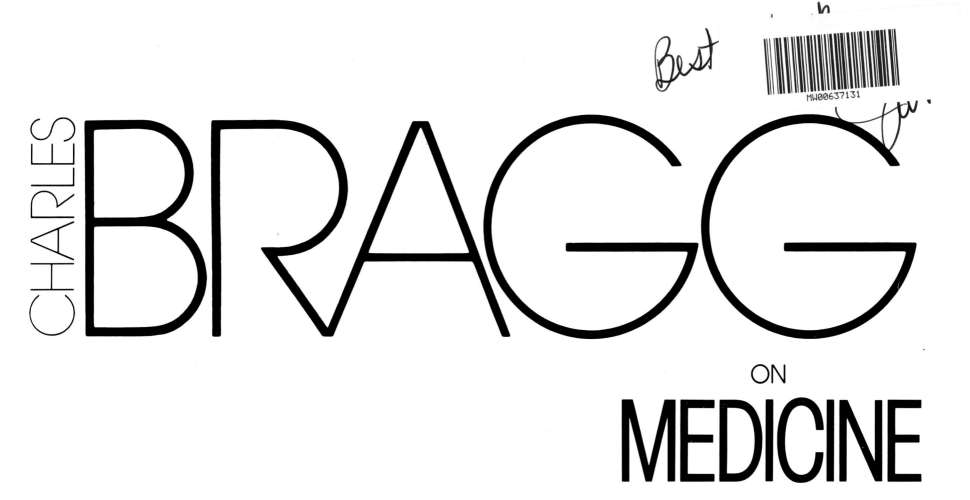

CHARLES BRAGG ON MEDICINE

Best *wish* *fu.*

CHARLES BRAGG

ON
MEDICINE

—Neurologist—

A sardonic view
of our fun-filled
medical system

35 images
by Charles Bragg

Introduction by
Pat McCormick

WARNER BOOKS

A Warner Communications Company

Printed in the United States of America
First printing: November 1984
10 9 8 7 6 5 4 3 2 1

Library of Congress Cataloging in Publication Data

Bragg, Charles.
  Charles Bragg on medicine.

  1. Medicine—Caricatures and cartoons.
2. American wit and humor, Pictorial. I. Title.
II. Title: Bragg on medicine.
NC1429.B733A4 1984a 741.5'973 84-7348
ISBN 0-446-38059-8 (pbk.) (U.S.A.)
     0-446-38060-1 (pbk.) (Canada)

Hippocrates the Greek physician who was Plato's doctor is generally considered to be the father of medicine. But he is dead and Plato's dead so how good a doctor could he have been?

Dealing everyday with life and death matters, a doctor of all people needs comic relief. Seeing the lighter side of medicine may very well be difficult for a doctor in the throes of his profession but not for Charles Bragg.

As a longtime friend I would hasten to establish that Charles Bragg is well qualified to comment on the field of medicine.

Here are a few of his credentials:

He worked his way through art school selling door to door Papp tests.

He knows that the leading symptom of bubonic plague is when a monk throws you on an ox cart.

You doubt Charles Bragg has a medical sense of humor? He sang "Ain't She Sweet?" at a diabetic convention.

Addressing a banquet of proctologists he accused them of lacking hindsight.

Charles Bragg willed his body to science and it was refused.

To save money, Bragg had his son circumsized at Benihana's.

Charles Bragg's family physician was upset because his lab monkeys died before he could give them cancer.

When a second opinion is needed, Bragg is crusading to get the first doctor a finder's fee.

Jennie Bragg, Charles' wife, sued Charles' sex therapist for malpractice...and collected.

He is no expert on medicine—he takes time release placebos. He lost money on the heat seeking suppository.

Medically speaking, your funny bone will be worn out enjoying Bragg's ribbing of the medical profession.

I leave you with this thought: What if the next surgeon to operate on Charles didn't think this book was funny?

Pat McCormick

"Every doctor in the world is a charlatan, except mine, who is a very wonderful man."
—*Mark Twain*

"In our specialized society we are so help-less in these people's hands. We depend on their expertise and feel so vulnerable. So I guess when I'm in my studio on my own turf it's my way of getting revenge. They are only human. They get speeding tickets and play bad bridge but sometimes that is hard to remember when you have appendicitis."
—*Charles Bragg*

"Like those of Bosch and Brueghel, the third B's canvases are crowded with a sky-burst of caricatures. Glimpsed through the refracting lens of his imagination, Bragg's world becomes an absurd one, peopled with gnome-like grotesques and oversized, puffy faces, beady eyes, bulbous noses and broken, jagged teeth.... He dips his brush or pen into the sinful universe and finds much to mock from the lofty to the lowly: politicians, lawyers, doctors, army generals, the hoi polloi. Not even the Pope is spared. And neither is Bragg."
—*Laurie Lucas,* <u>The Press-Enterprise,</u> *California*

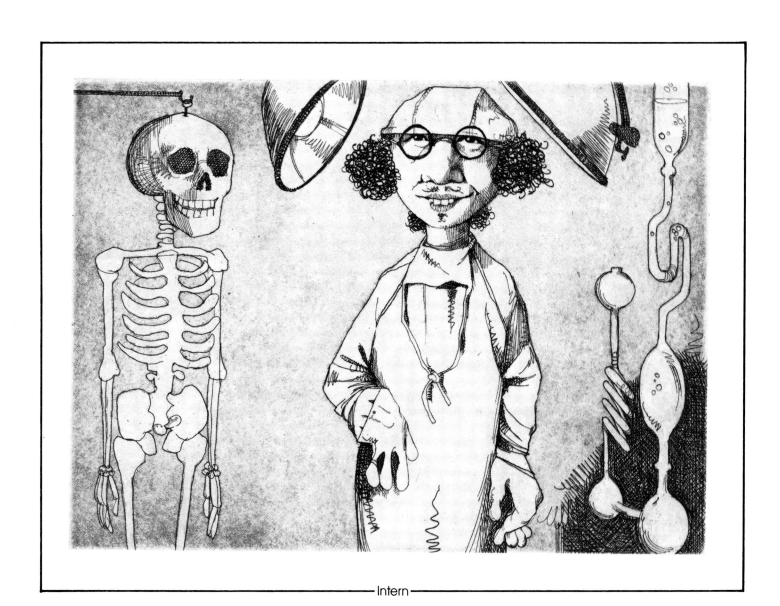

Intern

Visiting Hours

Psychiatrist

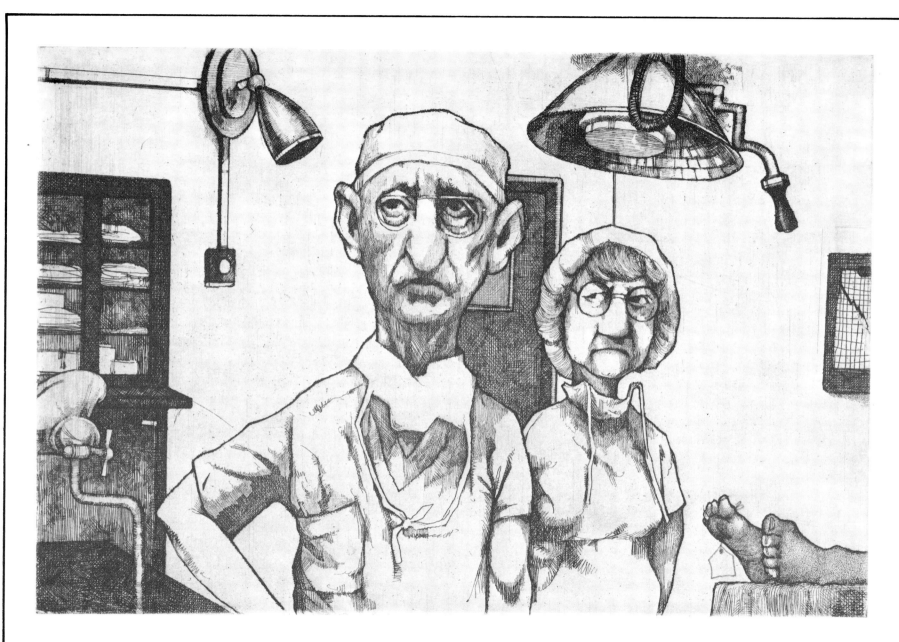

Recovery Room

Orthodontist

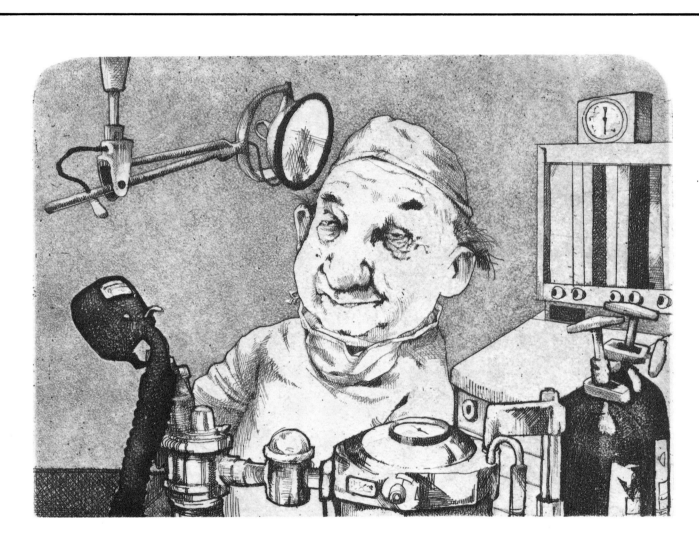

Anesthesiologist

G.P.

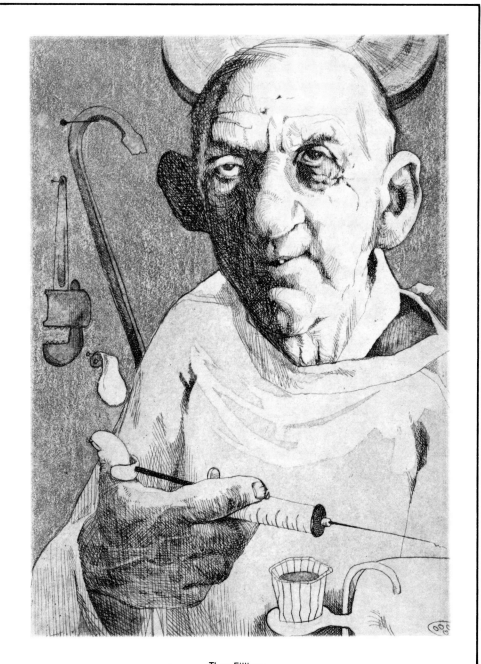

The Filling

Pediatrician

Researcher

Ophthalmologist

Neurologist

Brain Surgeon

Gynecologist

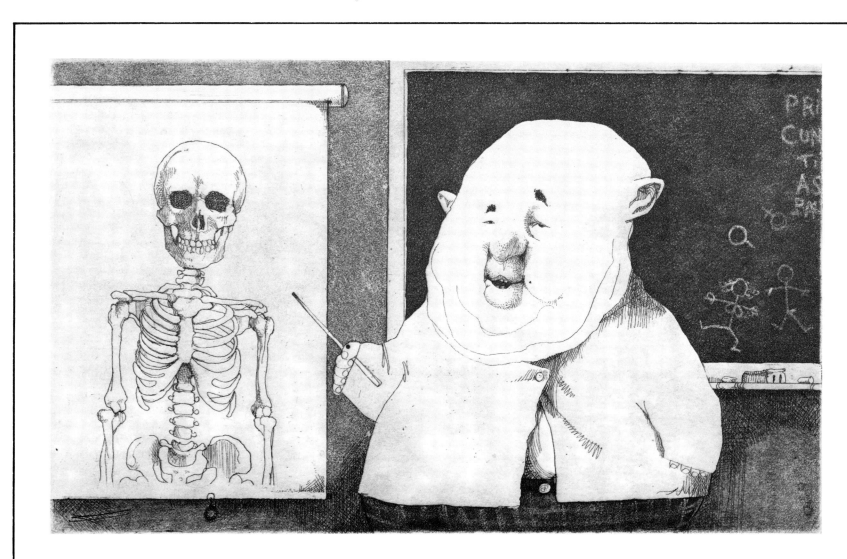

Anatomist

The First X-Ray

Compound Fracture

Angels of Mercy

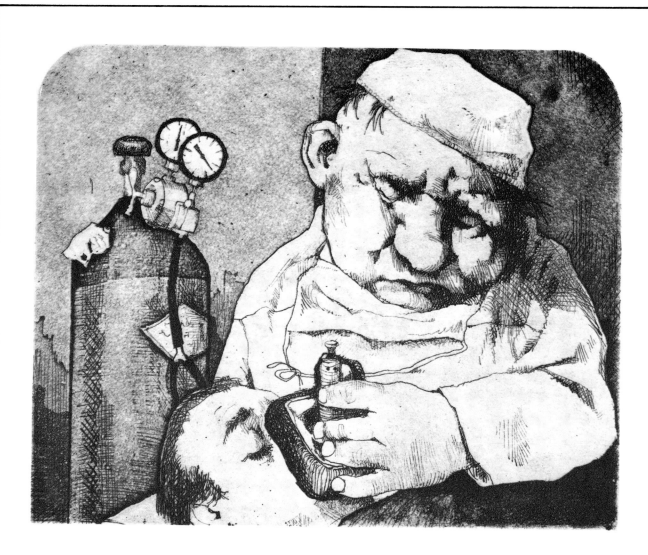

The Gas Man

Stress Test

Pharmacist

Psychiatrist

Surgeon

Urologist

Plastic Surgeon

Psychologist

Consultation

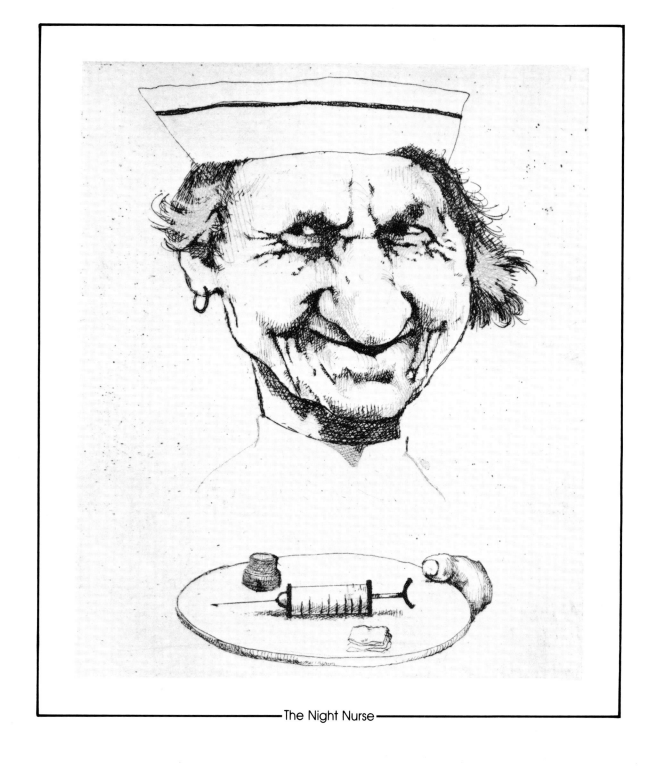

The Night Nurse

Gynecologist

Dr. Sneed

Doyle The Mohel

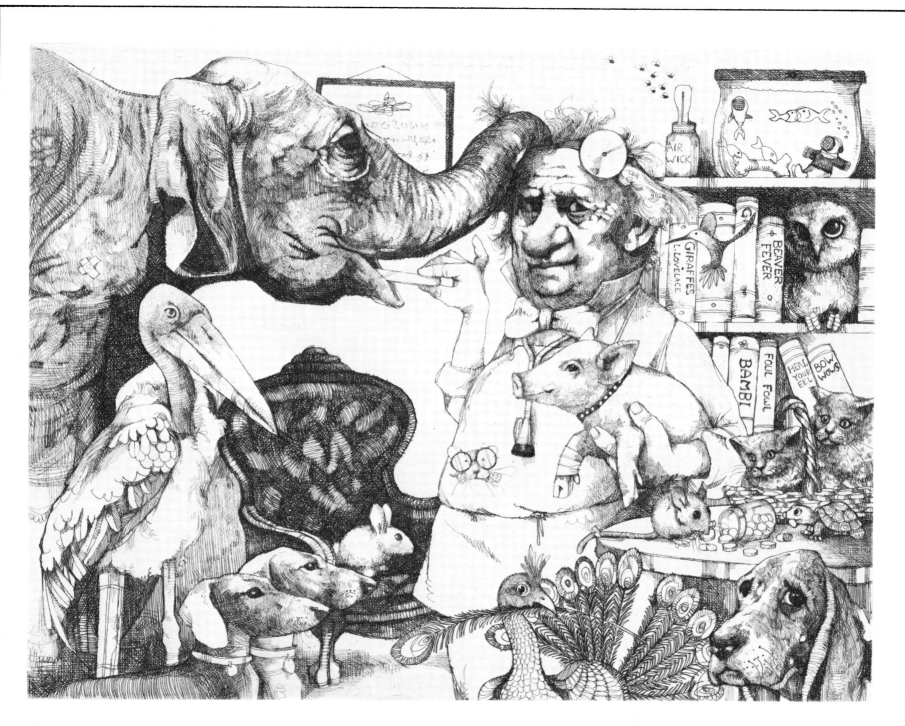

Veterinarian